Require
for the New Business Analyst

a quick start guide

The Simplified Beginners Guide to

Business Systems Analysis

By

Lane Bailey

Legal Notes

Introduction

In the early years of my career when I was a Business Analyst (BA), I had to fumble my way through many projects to learn the tools that I needed to be an effective BA. And then as a manager, I saw many new employees struggle because they weren't properly equipped for the role. But I didn't have the time or budget to send any of them to training. That's when I developed a simple three step process that I taught every new Business Analyst that joined my team. This process allowed me to train all new Business Analysts in ONE DAY, and get them effectively gathering requirements IMMEDIATELY. The feedback that I received was astounding. The employees were more confident in their role, and the stakeholders were very impressed at the skill of the new Business Analysts. But most importantly, they were able to produce and be effective right away.

This book is for anyone who is new to the Business Analyst role, someone looking to make a career change, or maybe even a veteran BA looking for a basic refresher. Either way, you'll walk away from this book with many tools to get you started the first day.

Table of Contents

Legal Notes

Introduction

Table of Contents

Chapter 1. The Vital Role of the Business Analyst

Overview of the Role 8

Overview of Project Management Methodologies 10

Waterfall 10

Agile 12

Chapter 2. BA Process Overview

Overview of the G.A.P. Methodology 15

Investigation 15

Gather 16

Analyze 16

Produce 16

Chapter 3. Gather

Investigation and Learning 17

Requirements Elicitation 23

Functional Requirements 25

Use Cases 29

Non Functional Requirements 33

Q&A 34

Chapter 4. Analyze

Review and Validate Requirements 37

Prioritize 37

Analyze for Clarity - Ensure Requirements are Unambiguous 37

Ensure Conciseness 38

Ensure Completeness 38

Assess for Feasibility 38

Determine Relevancy to Scope 39

Chapter 5. Produce

Business Problem Statement 42

Stakeholders 42

Terms and Definitions 43

Current Business Process 43

Scope Statement (in vs. out) 44

Key Business Objectives 46

Project Completion Criteria 46

Risks & Limitations 46

Assumptions 47

Functional & Non-Functional Requirements 48

Cost and scheduling parameters 48

New/Modified Business Process Flows 48

Training 49

Review and Approval Process 49

Q&A 51

Chapter 6. Manage Change

Q&A 54

Chapter 7. Conclusion and Next Steps

About The Author – Lane Bailey

Chapter 1. The Vital Role of the Business Analyst

Overview of the Role

Having a clear understanding of your role is the first step to being effective as a Business Analyst. The role expands well beyond just gathering requirements. Business Analysts are a liaison between the technology team and the business stakeholders. As a result, Business Analysts are often called upon to be champions of change, spearheading process improvement and technology development efforts for an organization.

Throughout the life of a project, you may be called upon to wear different hats. Your ability to remain flexible and open to taking on a number of tasks will not only help further your career, but it will make you an indispensable member of the team.

The skills needed for this role are wide ranging and include:

- An inquisitive nature

- Problem solving

- The ability to assimilate and process large amounts of data

- Quick learning

- Flexibility and open to change

- Public speaking

- Project Management

- Testing / Quality Assurance

What may surprise you is that these skills are not optional, in fact it is expected that as a Business Analyst, you are capable of ever single item on this list. Don't let that scare you though. I mention this because I don't want you to get frustrated when you are called upon to perform duties that you may think are outside your role or capabilities. Again, don't let it scare you. These are things that can be learned. Just be open and make the best of every situation you face during the course of a project.

So how do you learn all of this stuff you might ask? Well, honestly, there is no definitive way to prepare to for this role. Certainly there are tons of training classes, books, and online research that can give you a foundation. But I find that experience is the best teacher. That is why I developed the methodology that I am about to share with you in this book. It is designed to get you up and running as a Business Analyst from day one. Let's get started.

Overview of Project Management Methodologies

We will start our discussion with a quick overview of project management methodologies. A project methodology is nothing more than a series of steps or the process by which the project progresses from start to completion. Each step of the process is referred to as a project phase. It is important to understand each of these phases because you will be expected to participate and often lead at each phase of the project. The two main methodologies that you are likely to come across are Waterfall and Agile. There are some key differences between the two. And there are pros and cons to each. Let's take a look at each one.

Waterfall

In a Waterfall project, the project progresses in a very linear fashion. Each phase of the project is represented as a clear sequence of steps in that each preceding step must be completed before moving on to the next one. The phases of the Waterfall methodology are:

Conception – This phase involves a thorough assessment of the feasibility of the project. A cost vs. benefit analysis is often performed during this step. While this is primarily a task for the Project Manager, as a Business Analyst, you may be called upon to gather data such as cost estimates for this phase.

Initiation – During initiation, the project team is formed, and the objectives, scope, and deliverables of the project are defined. Your role here is to help with determining scope of the project. We'll talk more about that later.

Analysis – This is the phase where you will gather and document requirements. This is were the Business Requirements Document (BRD) is created.

Design – Once the BRD is complete. It is handed to the technical team to design a solution based on those requirements. Your role here is to answer questions from the technical team, manage any change to the requirements, and help prepare additional documentation for the project.

This documentation might include test plans, training manuals, process flows and checklists to represent the new process or system.

Construction – This is where the software team builds the solution. Again, your role here is to support the technical team and participate in the creation of other documents needed for the project.

Testing – The testing phase is where the solution is validated to ensure that it meets the requirements. This is usually a task for a separate Q&A team or someone who specifically performs that role. But as I mentioned earlier, that person could be you.

Deployment – Finally the solution is delivered and the users are trained on the new system or process. You may be called upon to provide some of the training or give presentations to other members of the organization explaining the new changes.

One of the challenges of this methodology is that it is often inflexible to change. Because each phase must be considered "complete" before moving on to the next, going back to previous phases is often very time consuming and costly. Also, because of this linear progression, there is often a very lengthy amount of time between definition of the requirements and the delivery of an actual solution. It is not uncommon for each phase in the Waterfall methodology to last for months. The result is often a solution that no longer meets the needs of the business or is inaccurate because they project team didn't gain valuable feedback from the stakeholders throughout the process. That's where the Agile methodology shines.

Agile

Agile is a software development methodology that allows project teams to be very flexible in accepting and acting upon the changing requirements of the business. Agile typically involves the delivery of the solution in small increments such that stakeholders have the opportunity to review and assess whether or not a solution truly addresses their needs. In addition, Agile is popular among many organizations because it actually delivers portions of the solution throughout regular intervals in the project. As a result, the stakeholders get the benefit of immediate results. And the development team can use this feedback to immediately correct course if necessary and deliver a new solution, often within a matter of a couple of weeks.

There is no right or wrong answer when it comes to which methodology is best. There are pros and cons to each. Some will argue that Waterfall is antiquated and should be abandoned altogether. But there are projects that could benefit from such a structured approach. For example a project involving a highly complex solution that may involve significant legal, regulatory, or financial implications. Right or wrong really isn't the scope of this book though. For now, it is important to simply be aware of the steps involved in each.

Plan of Action

Meet with the Project Manager to get an understanding of the following:

1. What is the core problem the project needs to solve?

2. The name and role of each stakeholder involved in the project

3. Which methodology the project is following?

4. Which phases you are expected to participate in, and what is your role in each?

5. What input and output are you expected to produce for each phase?

6. Get templates and examples for each deliverable you are responsible for. The Project Manager may have these or be able to direct you on how to get them. You can also ask other members of the project team, or reach out to a Business Analyst on another project.

7. Study and learn everything you have been given. Make a list of questions you have about

any of your deliverables. Meet with the Project Manager again to clear up any questions you have.

Chapter 2. BA Process Overview

Overview of the G.A.P. Methodology

I developed the G.A.P. methodology as a means to quickly get a brand-new business analyst up and running on a project. It is a quick and easy three step process that gets in analyst immediately engaged in the project and gives them the basics of what they need to start producing viable requirements for the project. I have had great success with this process. Many of my employees have told me how easy it was to follow this process and how much more confident they felt in gathering requirements. There are three steps involved in this process as follows:

1. Gather

2. Analyze

3. Produce

Let's get started exploring each.

Gather

In the gather phase you are acquiring all of the details about the business problem. You are collecting the stakeholder's requirements for the problem to be solved.

Analyze

During the analyze phase you will review the requirements for accuracy in preparation for the Business Requirements Document (BRD).

Produce

And finally in the produce stage of the process you're actually creating the BRD that will be used by the project team to build the solution to the business problem.

Next Steps

Let's get started on learning the G.A.P. Methodology. For each chapter, I have included a list of common questions that address issues you may face in your role as a Business Analyst. For many of these issues it is easy to simply escalate to the Project Manager. But please don't make that the default solution to the issues you face. If you want to be successful, you'll really want to try to solve many if not all of these items on your own if you can. I would suggest leaving the "escalate to Project Manager" as a last resort. Thus, I'll try to provide you with some tips to help solve some of these common problems.

The second thing that I want to mention is that you won't find any templates or checklists in this book. I like to focus on the "what" and the "why" behind the many facets of the role vs. "filling in the blanks" to templates. I believe that if you understand the theory behind the BA process, filling in any template will be the easy part.

Q&A

I just got pulled into a project that was already behind schedule and was told that I only have a few days to gather and document requirements. What do I do?

The first thing I would suggest is not to panic. This happens a lot unfortunately. One option would be to try to negotiate with the Project Manager for more time. If that is not an option, the first thing you will want to do is ask for a copy of any requirements that have already been gathered. You can use this as a starting point. And this will help you to determine how much is left to gather.

Spend time reviewing the requirements and validating them with each stakeholder. Then you can move on to using the method outlined in this book to collect and document any new requirements. Additionally, you want to document in your BRD the following items:

A) In the Limitations section of the BRD, note that there is a limit to the amount of requirements that can be gathered based on the limited timeline given for the task.

B) In the Risk section of the BRD, note that there is a risk that the system may not meet the full needs of the stakeholders as there was limited time to complete full requirements gathering.

Now, understand that just because you documented these two items, that does not give you a free ticket to limit what you can gather. You still want to give it your all to try to collect and document all requirements that you can within the time-frame allotted. Documenting these two items simply places all parties on the team on notice that the ultimate quality of the solution delivered may not meet the needs for which it is intended. Having it documented may just get you the additional time you need. Notice I said "may" get you extra time. It's not guaranteed. But I've always taught my BA's to document everything.

Chapter 3. Gather

A significant portion of your time as a BA will be gathering data. You'll then organize that data into a requirements document that the team will use to devise a solution to the business problem. Let's spend some time talking about the information you will need to gather, how to gather it, and where you can get that data. Before we get too much farther in talking about requirements, I want to address a key step that is so often overlooked in this process. And that step is the initial investigation and learning process.

Investigation and Learning

Although this is not a formal step in the G.A.P. methodology. It is really more of a precursor step, and a necessary one. It is easy to jump right into requirements meetings and start asking questions. But unless you know what questions to ask, you will simply be wasting your time. Unless you are already an expert or at least have some knowledge of the business process, you've got some work to do before you even start gathering requirements. You'll want to spend some time getting familiar with the process and systems that are being addressed by the project. You will need to know exactly what the process is, who is involved in the process, and you need to be able to clearly articulate the process (in business terms) to anyone involved in the project.

Your role as a Business Analyst is a very visible one. You are the liaison between the stakeholders and the technical team. The technical staff may approach you with questions, you may be asked to do a presentation to other departments, or you may need to answer questions from the Project Manager or the Q&A team. You'll want to be an authority in this area so that you don't have to run to the stakeholder for every little question that may come up. Just because you have a question doesn't mean your stakeholder is going to drop everything and come rushing to your aid with an answer. They are often very busy performing their normal job functions and may not even have time for the project at all beyond the initial requirements gathering. You don't want to hold up the process waiting for answers to simple questions that you as the authority should know.

Here are some other reasons why you don't want to skip this step:

1. You will learn to speak the language and learn the questions you need to ask during your requirements sessions

2. This is an opportunity to uncover hidden information that may not be common knowledge. Why is this important? Well, I've

seen entire sections of requirements become obsolete when a little known step clears up part of the problem. This happens quite often actually. Person A may do it one way, while Person B does it another. When they don't communicate, you end up with half of the staff encountering a problem that could be avoided if they simply switched how they performed the process. By simply communicating and retraining the staff on this step, they were able to solve half of the problem in question.

3. You'll gain credibility with the stakeholders. You want to be seen as knowledgeable. You want to project that you truly care about their problems. If you fail to gain credibility, you'll likely end up with stakeholders who won't participate because they don't believe that you are actually there to solve the problem anyway.

4. You want to gain allies and show that you are on their side. Of course this is supposed to be a team effort, but a surprising number of stakeholders feel that a project is a war or battle between them and the technology team. This happens largely due to lack of communication, failed projects, and many other political reasons that are beyond the scope of this document.

So as you spend your time learning about the business process there are several things you want to make sure you understand. First you want to understand how the process works from start to finish. You also want to know who performs the process, who provides input to the process, who receives output from that process. Systems and processes are not necessarily linear, so it is important to understand that there are multiple facets that comprise even one simple process. You also want to spend time learning the terms terms or lingo the stakeholders use in regards to their process or system.

So who exactly do you need to get this information from? The first place to start is the person who primarily performs that process on a daily basis. You also want to speak to the person or persons who provide input to the process or receive output from the process. The more people you speak with the more comprehensive your knowledge of the system process will be.

There are many ways to go about learning this information. You could spend time job shadowing and simply watching someone perform the process. You could ask your stakeholders for training manuals, perhaps you could attend training, and then of course there is one line research. The path to learning this information may not always be straightforward. Your job is to keep digging until you uncover all of the information that you need.

Plan of Action

1. Make a list of people you need to speak with to learn about the business process or system in question. Don't take your initial list at face value. Keep digging and asking around until you have a very comprehensive list of people to interview.

2. Schedule time with each person on your list. Explain to them that you want to take some time to learn their process, and ask if they would be willing to provide you with the information you need.

3. When you meet with each person, start by asking some of the questions listed below. Feel free to add any additional questions you feel necessary:

   1. What is your key objective when you perform this process?

   2. What determines if you have completed the process successfully?

3. Who else performs this process? Does everyone perform the same steps each time? If not, what are the differences?

4. Who or what provides input to this process? If so, what is the input? Can you provide me with samples of this input?

5. Who or what provides output to this process? If so, what is that output? Can you provide me with samples of this?

6. Who trained you on this process?

7. Do you have any training manuals that you can share with me? What about any job aids or checklists?

8. What are some of the problems you face in performing this process? Remember, you're not gathering requirements at this point. You're simply learning and building your knowledge.

4. Take detailed notes on the answers to each of these questions.

5. Study, and learn all material and information that has been shared with you. How do you know if you need further learning? If you are not able to answer "yes" to the following questions, keep digging:

1. Can you clearly and concisely explain the key business processes from start to finish?

2. Can you articulate who performs the process and what their main objectives are in performing the process?

3. Can you articulate some of the major pain points the users are experiencing with the process or system? Can you articulate how these problems are negatively impacting the business?

4. Can you articulate why this process is critical to the business?

Requirements Elicitation

So once you've completed your investigation and learning you are now ready to begin eliciting your requirements. Or in other words engaging with the stakeholders to determine their requirements for solution to their problem. So how do you go about getting these requirements? You will often need to use multiple methods to get the information you need.

Brainstorming Meetings

One of the most common methods to elicit requirements is brainstorming meetings and focus groups. A requirements meeting is often facilitated by you, the Business Analyst, and involves the participation of all stakeholders of project. During this meeting you'll ask key questions and and have detailed discussions about the requirements for the new system.

Document Analysis

Another method to eliciting requirements is document analysis. I've been on projects where we were given very limited time from the stakeholders. They simply gave us existing documents and training materials. This is not always the ideal way to go about capturing requirements, but it is one option.

Prototyping

Additionally business analyst will often then perform prototyping in order to elicit requirements.
Prototyping involves producing a very basic view of what the system might look like once complete. The prototype is not meant to be the actual solution. It is often very basic, crude, and contains very little more than screenshots that outline what a future system or process might look like. Prototypes are merely a tool that is used to facilitate discussion, encourage brainstorming, and encourage clear communication about what is required.

Surveys and Questionnaires

Another less frequent method to eliciting requirements is by the use of surveys and questionnaires. Based on information that you gather in your learning phase, you should be able to come up with a list of very specific questions that would lead you to fully understand the problem at hand. It will also help you to gain consensus on what exactly needs to be solved.

Functional Requirements

You'll often hear the terms functional requirements and nonfunctional requirements. There are some key differences between the two that we need to discuss before we move forward. A functional requirement defines what a system needs to do while the nonfunctional requirement defines how a system should perform something. For example:

- Functional Requirement - The system shall allow authorized users to delete student records

- Non-Functional Requirement - The system shall send an email to the System Administrator within 5 minutes of a student record being deleted

Functional requirements are usually written as "shall" statements that outline what the system must do. For example:

- The system shall allow authorized users to add new vehicles to the inventory

Organizing Requirements

As you move through this process, you will likely collect a fairly large number of requirements. You'll want to organize them in a way that makes it easy to document them and reference them in the requirements document. You could number them sequentially starting with number one ending with the number of requirements that you capture. Such as one, two, three,. A better approach however would be to come up with a methodical system to categorize and number your requirements. Here is one approach:

1. Categorize the requirements into sections for example: Email, Admin, or Marketing

2. Add the letters FR along with the category of the requirement, followed by the requirement number. For example: FR-Email-001 or FR-Admin-001

Plan of Action

1. Setup a requirements gathering meeting and invite each stakeholder.

2. Ask questions about the problem to be solved. Not all of these questions will be relevant, but it is a good start. The idea is to get you thinking so that you can come up with some questions on your own. Questions you will want to ask include:

    1. Describe in detail the problem to be solved

2. What has caused this problem?

3. Who experiences this problem?

4. When did this problem start?

5. How does the process work today?

6. Who provides input to the process ?

7. Who receives output from the process?

8. What would make the process easier to perform?

9. What are all systems are involved in this process?

   1. What system provides input?

   2. What system provides output?

10. What role does any of the input or output systems play in this problem?

11. How should the process work? Describe in detail the ideal process

12. Are there any other parties that need to be involved in solving this problem? (If they say yes, you'll need to meet with them to gather their requirements)

3. Take detailed notes during these discussions. Remember, you are collecting data to build

the Requirements Specification that is the foundation of the project. Gather as much information as you can to ensure that your requirements are complete.

1. Build a list of requirements that follow the pattern of: The system shall [do what]?

2. Label and number each requirement

Non Functional Requirements

So as we discussed earlier a nonfunctional requirement defines how a system will perform a certain action. It also further defines the performance characteristics of the system such as accessibility, efficiency, reliability, response time, and quality. Remember this is a non-technical document, so these types of requirements are still obtained from your stakeholders. It's tempting to want to gather these requirements from the technical staff when you see words such as reliability and response time. But remember that this is not a technical document. It is a business document. Therefore your stakeholders are the ones who need to outline their requirements for These items. You should each non-functional requirement as "shall" statements as we talked about earlier. And you'll number them in the same manner. Here are some examples of nonfunctional requirements:

- The system shall send a notification to the System Administrator for every failed login attempt.

- The system shall log the user out after 15 minutes of activity.

Plan of Action

1. Schedule a meeting with your stakeholders

2. Ask some of the following questions to build a list of non-functional requirements:

   1. What is the expected response time of the system in this process?

   2. What are the availability requirements for the system. For example 24 hours per day, or 8am-5pm, etc.

3. Build a list of requirements that follow the pattern of: The system shall [do what]?

Use Cases

so you may have heard the term use case along with a myriad of descriptions or definitions of a use case. It can get confusing, so I'll provide a very brief and basic definition of a use case. A use case is simply a textural representation of a process the user performs to accomplish a task. It documents how a user interacts with a system to achieve a specific goal. A use case is primarily textual, and can be accompanied by process flow or what is known as a use case diagram. For the purposes of this book, we will only address textual use cases. But I will have a book coming out very soon that dives deeper into use cases and use case diagrams.

Use cases are important because they provide very clear nontechnical overview of the process and user interaction with the system to perform the process. A use case is something that is written to be understood by every member of the project. Use cases do not outline any technical details pertaining to the system. They only contain steps describe the user interaction with the system. Another important point is that these use cases should be "future state" use cases. Meaning you want to outline the process as the business envisions it when the project is complete.

So how do you come up with use cases? Well as a start you would revisit all of the information that you learned during your investigation process. Revisit all those process flows and start to identify processes that will need to be described in your use cases. Keep in mind that although you may have learned information about several processes. Use cases used for your requirements document should be processes that are relevant to the project. So let's talk about some of the different components that make up a use case.

Actors

An actor is someone performing a specific role who uses the system to accomplish a specific task. Actor names are not necessarily tied to job titles. They are simply roles that a person performs while utilizing the system. For example Buyer, Seller, Investigator

Preconditions

A precondition is anything that is assumed to be true or available before the use case can begin. For example if you had a use case for a customer withdrawing money from an ATM. One of the preconditions would be: The ATM has cash available

Happy Path

The happy path is the series of steps that lead to a successful interaction to accomplish one goal in the system. It does not address any errors that occur along the way. Happy path only addresses the successful most straightforward path through a process.

Exception path

The exception path outlines the process that a user follows when an error occurs through the normal execution of that process.

Alternate Path

the alternate path is a lesser common system interaction such as resetting the password.

So what makes a good solid use case? Want to make sure that your use case has a clear starting point. It should also have a clear endpoint. A good use case has clearly defined actors. And it does not mix error and alternate path in the same use case.

Plan of Action

1. Meet with your stakeholders

2. Define the actors. Remembers, these are not job titles. They are roles that the user plays in the process or when working with the system.

3. Outline the steps required to define the ideal/future state of the process.

4. Use these steps to start building your use cases. There may be many roles involved in this process. You may want to do one use case per role (unless of course they participate in the same process to perform a task)

5. Continue working with your stakeholders until you have collected all use cases. Be sure to review each use case with them to ensure that it is accurate. This may take several meetings to get everything documented.

Q&A

My stakeholders aren't cooperating. They never seem to have time to answer my questions. My documents are due now. What do I do?

This is never an easy situation. The initial thought you may have is that you don't want to say anything because you don't want to get anyone "in trouble" so to speak. This is understandable, but at the same time, you have a job to do. The first course of action would be to see why this person never has time for you. Maybe it is a scheduling conflict, perhaps it is a lack of understanding of why they are needed, or perhaps they don't fully understand the value of the project. So before you write this person off as a problem maker, it would help to understand the underlying issue that maybe you can solve or workaround. Your objective is to be an ally and a good team member. If you can solve a problem for them, perhaps you will get a bit more cooperation. The next option would be to see if there is someone else that can replace this stakeholder. Perhaps there is someone else with just as much knowledge who can help out. However, you may do all of this and still have no success. Sometimes there is just no avoiding escalating things to your Project Manager. Ultimately that is what they are there for. To help resolve issues so that you can be successful.

I can sense that some stakeholders aren't sharing the true process. What do I do?

Again, you will need to dig in order to find the underlying cause of this issue. I've found that sometimes people hold back on sharing information because they fear that the new solution will make their job obsolete. While that may or may not be the case, you still need whatever information they may have for your BRD. In this case, you may have to gather information from multiple people who may have this information. Its not ideal, but you may be able to piece together the full details of what you need. This is also where you want to refer back to any materials you may have gathered in your Investigation and Learning stage. If you've exhausted all options, it may be time to escalate to the Project Manager.

I can't get everyone to agree on a particular requirement. What do I do?

This is not always a bad thing. You want stakeholder involvement and feedback. The fact that they are disagreeing means they are engaged in the process and more than likely care about getting it right. You'll have to put on your referee hat and your negotiator hat for this one. First of all, have the parties who disagree outline in detail the reason for their disagreement. Next, ask them if there is any part of the requirement they can agree on. If so, that's half the battle. Now you just have to focus on the item in question. Is it a wording issue? Is the requirement missing information from it? Does it have too much information in it, thereby making it confusing? Is the disagreement over whether or not the requirement is even needed? You'll need to continue to work with the parties involved to get to the bottom of the issue. Usually if you take the time to work through it, this sort of thing works itself out.

I think I have too many requirements. My BRD is huge! How do I know if I have too many? What do I do about it?

The only way to know this is by performing all of the steps outlined in the Analyze phase that we'll discuss in an upcoming chapter. If there are truly unnecessary or "too many" requirements in the document, they can usually be attributed to things such as requirements not being defined clearly enough, out of scope, or a myriad of other things we'll discuss shortly.

Nobody shows up to my requirements elicitation meetings. What do I do?

I'll give the same advice that I gave earlier for stakeholders who don't make time for you. The same principles apply. Remember, be an ally and a good team member. Try to figure out what is keeping them from participating and try to help make it easier for their participation.

Chapter 4. Analyze

The analyze phase is where you really start to finalize requirements into something that is tangible and ready to be shared. During this phase you are going to spend a lot of time reviewing and validating each and every requirement that you have gathered. Review and validation is important because you want to ensure that what you have captured accurately represents requirements that the stakeholders have given you. It gives the stakeholders an opportunity to make any revisions, clarifications, or if necessary additions to the requirements. This is also the step where you ensure that everyone on the project team is on the same page about requirements.

For each requirement you will evaluate them against a list of criteria to be sure that they are ready to be included in your requirements document. Reviews can happen in group meetings, one-on-one reviews, and even email reviews. Although you can do email reviews it really is not a preferred method. You really want to spend time face-to-face with your stakeholders thoroughly reviewing the document so that you can both immediately address any issues or questions that may arise.

The requirements should be documented, actionable, measurable, testable, traceable, related to identified business needs or opportunities, and defined to a level of detail sufficient for system design.

Review and Validate Requirements

Here you will review the requirements with the entire project team. This review should address the correctness and validity of each requirement. It also serves as an opportunity for additional input or feedback.

Prioritize

it's easy for the stakeholders to simply tell you that they want everything on the requirements lists. And while the goal may certainly be to provide all of those items, you want to get them to elaborate which ones are of highest priority, and which ones can be addressed later in the project. You may run across stakeholders who may have a difficult time prioritizing or they simply refuse to do so for fear that they won't get everything on their list. I will cover some tips in the Q&A section on how to deal with this. The most important thing to note at this point is that you want to get a clear definition of high priority items, medium priority items, and low priority items.

Analyze for Clarity - Ensure Requirements are Unambiguous

Each requirement should be clearly written in a manner such that requirement can only be interpreted in the manner in which it was intended. There should be no question as to what the requirement means. If you find that there are differing opinions or definitions of the purpose of a specific requirement, you need to revisit that item rewrite it to be more clear. If you fail to do this, not only do you run the risk of delivering a solution that does not solve the problem, it wastes time due to rework, and it makes it harder to determine success of the project.

Ensure Conciseness

Best practice here is to keep your sentences short and written with simple easy to understand language.

Ensure Completeness

For each requirement, you'll want to determine if it completely captures the requirement in question.

Assess for Feasibility

Is it a requirement that can be delivered? You will want to work with your entire project team to help answer this question.

Determine Relevancy to Scope

You also want to make sure that each requirement is relevant to the scope of the project. Stakeholders will often get excited making a list of requirements and attempt to accomplish everything on their problem list, even if it doesn't relate to the project. But you want to make sure that you limit your requirements to only those that are within the scope of the project.

Plan of Action

Review your requirements in detail. For every requirement, check it against the criteria outlined in this chapter as follows:

1. Is the requirement clear?

2. Is it unambiguous?

3. Is it written in a concise manner

4. Is it complete?

5. Is it feasible?

6. Is it relevant to the scope of the project?

Q&A

My stakeholders are having a hard time prioritizing the requirements. To them, everything is "High" priority and needs to be done right away

This is a common problem. Often the source of the problem is fear. I've seen stakeholders so afraid that they won't get anything marked lower than a "High" priority, that they refuse to even consider prioritizing anything. A lot of times, this is just a lack of understanding. You need to help them to understand that prioritizing anything lower than "High" does not mean that it won't get done. It just simply outlines the order in which they would like the project team to address the requirements. You may need to involve others in this discussion, to help ease their fears.

Chapter 5. Produce

The Business Requirements Document (BRD) is a key document that serves as a means of communication between the business and technology provider. This document holds the information that you worked so tirelessly to collect in the Gather phase. It's ultimate purpose is to

1. Describe what the solution must do to solve the business problem or meet the business need

1. Gain agreement among stakeholders

An important note worth mentioning is that this document focuses on the solution from the business perspective. It is not meant to describe technical function. This is a key point that is often either confused or overlooked. I've seen many new Analysts loose sight of this fact, and end up with a document that ends up hurting the project team more than helping the project team. This problem happens so easily, that its often hard to spot until it is too late.

It can happen one of two ways, sometimes both. One, the business is so close to the process and has often been dealing with the problem for so long, that they may already have a solution in mind. So what comes out in the requirements gathering phase often ends up being a "wish list" of screens and process that represents how they believe the problem should be solved. I've seen stakeholders show up to elicitation meetings with full mock-ups of their solution. While this can be helpful, this stage of requirements is not meant to capture this level of detail.

The other way the BRD ends up being too technical is when the technology team gets involved in the early stages of requirements gathering. The developers are often glad to be involved in this stage of the project. But they can get wrapped up in designing solutions right in the middle of the requirements meetings. And once the topic of discussion veers off in that direction, it is hard to reign it back in. I'll talk about a few ways to handle this in a bit.

The BRD also serves as the input to several other project management documents such as the Test Plan, Training Manuals, etc. So let's get started looking at the key sections of the BRD. Depending on the BRD template you are using, some of these sections may be labeled differently or not included at all. The below list just outlines some of the common sections.

Business Problem Statement

The Problem Statement outlines the nature of the problem to be solved. It is written from a business perspective and illustrates the so called "pain" the stakeholders have been facing that needs addressing. This should be a clear and concise paragraph that summarizes the problem.

Stakeholders

A stakeholder is someone who has a vested interest in the successful completion of the project. Stakeholders can be further defined by answering the following question: "Who do I need to talk to in order to understand the problem and define the requirements?" This can get a little tricky to define, because some new analysts make the mistake of only defining a stakeholder as the person who is sponsoring the project. This is not the only type of stakeholder that needs to be considered. When you fail to identify all stakeholders, you'll end up with a requirements document that only partially addresses the problem, or worse negatively impacts a stakeholder who was left out of the process. To ensure that doesn't happen, be sure to address some of the following to find your stakeholders:

- Other teams who may be impacted by the new solution

- External business partners

- Upper level management

- Technical staff such as Systems Administrators and Database Administrators. Often these people are not a part of the project directly, but may be called upon to support the project in some way or to answer technical questions in regards to the current state of the system or process.

As I mentioned earlier, it is important to note that you want to get specific names of people for your stakeholder list. Don't just list "The Accounting Department" for example. You want to get very specific as in "Tom Wilson, Accounting Department Manager".

Terms and Definitions

This is an area where you can't assume everyone is on the same page. You'll want to define any terms and definitions that are specific to the business problem being solved. Sure, you may know what "Accrual Method" means, but does everyone else on the team? If not, it could lead to inaccurate requirements.

Current Business Process

This section of the document specifies the business process as it stands currently. Typically these would be represented with Process Flow diagrams. These are created with programs such as Microsoft Visio and to some extent (and with limited capabilities) Microsoft

PowerPoint. Creation of these flows is beyond the purpose of this book. I'll have a future book that delves more deeply into some of these deliverables. But for now, I think it is sufficient to know the basics to get you started as quickly as possible.

Scope Statement (in vs. out)

A scope statement describes what exactly the solution should and should not address. And believe it or not, the "not included" is just as (and sometimes more) important than the "should be included. Let me explain what I mean.

Often, the stakeholders have been suffering a great deal of so called "pain" because of the problem they are facing. When IT gets involved to solve it, the stakeholders get so excited that they try to throw in everything imaginable. Even requirements that address other problems they may be facing. When this happens, the scope of the project gets so big that it becomes unclear when the project is actually finished. It gets confusing to the developers. It makes Q&A a monumental task, the Project Manager gets frustrated trying to manage so many deliverables. And a project with a large scope can get very expensive very quickly. Overall, a large scope is a nightmare to everyone involved in the project.

You'll need to work with your stakeholders to commit to a very clear and concise scope statement for the project. This is often not easy to do, as they'll want to squeeze in as much as they can. Check out the Q&A section below for some tips on how to handle when you can't get your stakeholders to commit to a reasonable scope.

Key Business Objectives

This section of the document outlines the overall objectives the project is addressing. What does the project hope to accomplish?

Project Completion Criteria

What determines when the project is complete? How does the project team know they have delivered what the business has requested? This is why it is so important to get a solid scope statement defined. That scope statement feeds right into this section of the document. You'll need to define up front with the stakeholders what criteria must be met to consider the project "Complete".

Risks & Limitations

With every project, there are risks and limitations involved. Some risks to think about include:

- There is a risk that the ABC system may not be compatible

- There is a risk that there will not be enough physical space for the new hardware

Assumptions

If you've ever heard the saying about making assumptions, you'll need to forget about it for this section of the document. You never, I repeat never want anything to be assumed when you are dealing with a project and an entire team of people who need to be on the same page. You'll want to document exactly what should be assumed as a part of this project. Some examples of assumptions that you might want to think about include:

- o Resources from other teams will (or will not) be involved for the duration of the project

- o The stakeholders will make members of their staff available throughout the project during a certain time period of the day (8am-12pm or only 12pm-2pm etc.)

- o The stakeholders will approve what is delivered at the end of the project. I know this should be a given, but trust me, it's not. I've seen stakeholders refuse to approve at the completion of the project even though they may agree the solution fully and successfully meets their needs. Get clear up front on who is responsible for signing-off the project once it is complete.

Functional & Non-Functional Requirements

This is a big chunk of the document that is pretty much complete if you've properly gathered your requirements as we've discussed earlier. Here is where you'll include your requirements list, use cases, and business rules.

Cost and scheduling parameters

This is where you will outline the budget for the project, who is managing the budget, and what happens in the case of cost overruns. Also, this is where you outline the high-level timeline for the project. Essentially, just the major milestone dates.

New/Modified Business Process Flows

This is pretty self explanatory. These process flows should outline the business process as it will look at the completion of the project. Again, this is documented purely from the business perspective. These process flows should not mention any technical solution or even a hint at system design. What you want here is simply business process.

Training

This section is where you'll specify things such as what type of training is needed for the new solution. Also, who will provide training, how will training will be provided, how much training is to be provided, and when will it be provided. You'll also want to know if it is included in the project budget or will it be paid for outside the project.

Review and Approval Process

This is where you will outline the procedures for the review and approval of the BRD. Some questions to consider are:

- who needs to review it?

- Who needs t sign it?

- How will approval be performed?

Plan of Action

I have good news for you. If you've followed the G.A.P. Methodology, you should already have over 80% of the information needed for building the BRD. All you have left to do is:

1. Input the data you've gathered into the relevant sections of the document.

2. Meet with anyone you need to help fill in any blanks you may have.

3. Get approvals on the document to signify that it is complete and ready to be used for the remaining phases of the project. This may sound like a straightforward and easy process. But I have often found out that getting approval on this document can be downright frustrating. I tell you that to not to scare you, but to prepare you. I hope you don't run into issues at this stage. But there are a few things you may face at this stage.

    1. One of the stakeholders has found something wrong in the document and it needs to be corrected before they will approve.

    2. One of your stakeholders may not be available to provide approval

    3. Your stakeholders may have to review the document with their managers before signing off.

This is all worth noting because it may take days, and sometimes even weeks to get everyone to approve the document. I'll discuss some tips below on how to handle some of these scenarios.

Q&A

My stakeholders won't commit to signing-off on the BRD. What do I do?

Again, you'll need to get to the core reason of why they won't sign off. If it is simply due to additional corrections, then you should go ahead and make the changes, as long as the changes don't impact the agreed upon scope. If however there other reasons keeping them from signing-off, this may be a good time to involve the Project Manager.

The stakeholders keep making changes to the document even though we've reviewed several times. What do I do?

I find that when this happens, usually the underlying cause is that there is a problem with the quality of the requirements. I would suggest you revisit the items outlined in Chapter 5 to ensure that your requirements are clear, concise, and complete. Also, it would help if they are written in short sentences, and in a language that everyone can understand. Avoid big words, slang, or jargon that is not common knowledge. Keep it as simple as possible.

The requirements are done, but the key stakeholder won't approve them, even though they have agreed that the requirements are accurate. What do I do?

There are many reasons why a stakeholder won't approve the final BRD. It might be fear of committing to something that may "fail" and they don't want their name on it. Or it could simply be due to a misunderstanding or disagreement about something in the document. Try to get to the bottom of what's keeping them from signing-off. The issue may be simpler than you think.

Chapter 6. Manage Change

So your requirements document has been approved, what are your next steps. What is your role on the remainder of the project? One of the key items that you will be responsible for is change management. Change is inevitable. Requirements change, the timeline can change, expectations change. It is up to you to document the change and help the team to manage the change.

There are many things that will need to be updated as the project progresses. Things such as training materials, checklists, work aids, and even requirements. The one thing probably most important thing that I really want addresses a part of this change management process is how you manage change in requirements. Oftentimes we think that changing requirements during the middle project is automatically a bad thing. But that's just not the case. In fact if your project is following an agile methodology, you should welcome change. Not all change is bad. The change in requirements is good because a it will allow you to correct course if you notice that the solution is not meeting or going to meet the business need. Be it is also good because you get quicker feedback from your stakeholders.

So what do you do when one of your stakeholders comes to you with a requirements change? The first thing you want to do is to determine why the requirement needs to change in the first place. Was it captured incorrectly during requirements gathering? Is it something new that they realize needs to be addressed in order to solve the problem? Is it the removal of a requirement? Or is your stakeholders simply trying to throw in a bunch of items at the last minute? You need to work very closely with the stakeholder, the project manager, and the rest of the project team to determine the impact this requirement change will have on the project. Not only that, you will want to fully understand the impact of the change so that you can make the stakeholder aware of any timeline or budgetary impacts it could have. If a requirements change has been approved, it is your job as the business analyst update the requirements document. Any time you make a change to the requirements document after it has been approved, you will need to hold another review and validation session with your stakeholders, and receive new approval.

Plan of Action

1. Remain flexible at this stage. Things will change. Try not to get frustrated.

2. Ask the Project Manager what the procedures are for making a change

3. If you do encounter any changes, make sure you review it with the entire team before making the change. In addition, you may need to get the stakeholders to approve the updated documentation.

Chapter 7. Conclusion and Next Steps

I believe we have covered everything that you need to get started on your role as a Business Analyst. I hope that the G.A.P. Methodology provides you with the tools you need to be effective in your role right away. As I said earlier, I believe experience is the best teacher. Keep working at it. The BA role is not an easy one. You are required to wear many hats and accomplish many things, often under tight time-lines. Just keep working at it, keep asking questions, and try to keep a smile on your face as you navigate the many facets of a project. Best of luck!

About The Author – Lane Bailey

Lane Bailey is a self proclaimed IT fanatic. He has over 17 years of experience that spans both the software and hardware side of technology. His expertise includes the design and building of new software systems, conversion of legacy systems, process analysis and design. He has held numerous roles including IT Manager, Network Analyst, Software Engineer, Business Systems Analyst and Software Trainer. Lane holds an Associates in Business degree and a Bachelor of Information Technology degree. Throughout his career, he has helped companies with process and software implementations that have resulted in over $200 million dollars in savings and cost avoidance.

Made in the USA
Las Vegas, NV
29 November 2022

60664413R00039